ROME

ROME

914.5632

KAREN FARRINGTON

ERRATA

The publisher would like to point out amendments to
the following pages of this book.

Page 7, line 3: the word should be visitors, not trippers.

Page 7, paragraph 2, next to last line: should be…and you are walking where…

Page 18, paragraph 1, line 1: should be, Augustus was also in the habit of writing.
Below he…

Page 20, last sentence of paragraph 5: should read…were devastating, with
much of Rome looted.

Page 26, caption: should be designed by Bernini (not Bernine).

Page 26, paragraph 3, line 1: should be Raphael (not Rahael).

Page 60, caption for Above: in two instances should read Bernini (not Bermini).

GRAMERCY BOOKS
NEW YORK

This 2000 edition is published by Gramercy Books™,
a division of Random House Value Publishing, Inc.,
280 Park Avenue, New York, NY 10017.
by arrangement with PRC Publishing Ltd, London.

Kiln House, 210 New Kings Road, London SW6 4NZ

Gramercy Books™ and design are registered trademarks of
Random House Value Publishing, Inc.
Random House
New York • Toronto • London • Sydney • Auckland
http://www.randomhouse.com/

Printed and bound in China
A CIP catalogue record for this book is available from the Library of Congress.

ISBN 0-517-16176-1

8 7 6 5 4 3 2 1

ACKNOWLEDGMENTS
The publisher wishes to thank the following for supplying the photography for this book:

Pictor International - London for pages 2, 33, 36, 44-45 (main), 47, 53, 56,
57, 58-59, 62-63, 64, 65, 78-79, 90-91, 92-93, 97, 98, 99, 100-101, 102-
103, 106-107, 111, 116-117, 118, 119 and 126-127 (main);
© Charles & Josette Lenars/CORBIS for pages 6, 37 and 54-55;
© Peter Wilson/CORBIS for pages 9 and 25;
© Ruggero Vanni/CORBIS for pages 10, 13 and 17;
© Macduff Everton/CORBIS for page 14;
© Vince Streano/CORBIS for page 18;
© Michael S Yamashita/CORBIS for pages 21, 40, 43, 121 and 122-123
(main);
© Gianni Dagli Orti/CORBIS for page 22;
© John Heseltine/CORBIS for pages 26, 50, 61, 66, 88, 105, 112 and 120;
© Kelly-Mooney Photography/CORBIS for pages 29 and 125;
© Underwood & Underwood/CORBIS for page 30;
© Hubert Stadler/CORBIS for pages 34, 83 and 86;
© Julian Calder/CORBIS for pages 35 and 124;
© Dave G Houser/CORBIS for page 38;
© David Lees/CORBIS for page 39;
© Francesco Venturi; Kea Publishing Services Ltd./CORBIS for pages 41,
74-75 (top), 76, 81, 84, 85 and 122 (left);
© Owen Franken/CORBIS for pages 42 and 94;
© Hugh Rooney; Eye Ubiquitous/CORBIS for pages 45 (inset, right) and
108;

© Massimo Listri/CORBIS for pages 46 and 77;
© Vanni Archive/CORBIS for pages 48, 60, 70-71 and 89;
© Archivo Iconografico, S.A./CORBIS for page 49;
© Andrea Jemolo/CORBIS for page 51;
© HorreeZirkee Produk/CORBIS for page 52;
© Carmen Redondo/CORBIS for page 67;
© Dennis Marsico/CORBIS for pages 68 (left), 73 and 74 (left);
© Franz-Marc Frei/CORBIS for pages 68-69 (main);
© Adam Woolfitt/CORBIS for page 72;
© Robert Holmes/CORBIS for page 80;
© Araldo de Luca/CORBIS for page 82;
© Jan Butchofsky-Houser/CORBIS for page 87;
© Vittoriano Rastelli/CORBIS for pages 95 and 114;
© Stephanie Colasanti/CORBIS for page 96;
© Angelo Hornak/CORBIS for pages 104 and 110;
© Sandro Vannini/CORBIS for page 109;
© Fotografia, Inc./CORBIS for page 113;
© Peter Turnley/CORBIS for page 115;
© Francis G Mayer/CORBIS for page 127 (right).

For jacket image acknowledgments see inside flap.

Page 2

Enjoying a break at one of the Piazza Navona's cafés.

CONTENTS

INTRODUCTION

With the elegance of London, the romance of Paris, the commercial significance of Berlin, and the conviviality of Amsterdam, Rome is a must-see city. It is a magnet for trippers who are awed at its architectural splendor and enchanted by street theater, sunshine dappled through the leaves of a caper tree, and the roadside symphony of honking horns. City dwellers, frustrated by traffic jams or outraged by slap-dash service and political instability, take a different view. Yet no one who knows Rome remains unaffected by her. The sheer unstoppable magic of the place streams along the streets in the wake of noisy Lambrettas and bursts forth from majestic fountains.

Rome is a city marked by time. It has a modern face commensurate with any national capital. This is the seat of Italy's government and the headquarters of such institutions as the United Nations Food and Agriculture Organization and the World Food Program. A host of buildings went up during the preparations for the 1960 Olympics, from where the first ever live TV broadcast in the history of the Games was made—in black and white, of course. (Ribbons and chains for medals also made their first appearance here.) Just 30 years earlier, the city was being re-fashioned by Fascist leader Mussolini. Strip away more layers, and you discover Baroque and Renaissance jewels. Slip back further, and you are walk where Roman emperors, legionnaires, and slaves once trod.

Beneath all that has been wrought by humanity stand the Seven Hills of Rome—Capitoline, Quirinal, Viminal, Esquiline, Celian, Aventine, and Palatine (there are other hills in the landscape, notably Pincio—now known for its park—and Janiculum). With this knowledge alone it is possible to begin navigation of the area. The hills lay clustered before a ford in the River Tiber, the last before its opening into the Mediterranean Sea, which once had all the makings of a natural port.

Left:

Balconies

Rome is a feast of architectural beauty for visitors. For its residents the cramped conditions of some quarters, traffic fumes, and the seasonal sweltering sunshine are a way of life.

Rome's geographic advantages were apparent to first settlers. Roman historian Livy (59AD–17AD) explained in his *History of Rome*:

"Not without good reason did gods and men select this place for founding a city: these most healthful hills; a commodious river, by means of which the produce of the soil may be conveyed from the inland countries, by which maritime supplies may be obtained; close enough to the sea for all purposes for convenience and not exposed by too much proximity to the dangers of foreign fleets; a situation in the center of the regions of Italy, singularly adapted by nature for the increase of a city."

Its history, in fact, begins in the dark recesses of time. Myth has it that the city in the region of Latium was founded by Romulus on April 21, 753BC. He and his brother Remus were twin sons of Princess Rhea Silvia, born after she had been raped by Mars, the god of war. They were cast adrift on the River Tiber in a wooden chest by a jealous uncle, rescued and suckled by a she-wolf (some believe it was actually a local whore with the nickname of Wolf), and finally adopted by a shepherd. Romulus rose to be a tribal leader and began to build a city on what we now know as Palatine Hill. Remus made a fatal error in mocking his brother's constructions: Romulus killed him and thereafter ruled unopposed. So brutal was he that, when he decided he and his comrades were short of women, he kidnapped and raped the females of the neighboring Sabine tribe. Romulus was apparently murdered too, despite his close links to the gods, the first but by no means the only leader of Rome to meet a grisly end.

Legends are a giant leap away from truth, but we do know that Rome was home for some ancient peoples eight centuries before Christ and perhaps even earlier. Traces of their daub and wattle huts and similarly shaped funeral urns have been uncovered to prove this.

With Romulus' successors it is difficult to distinguish between fact and fantasy, but for the record, their names were Numa Pompilius, Tullus Hostilius, and Ancus Martius. The first bridge across the Tiber, the wooden Sublicius bridge built in about 650BC, is generally attributed to the latter, as is occupation of the Aventine and Janiculum hills.

Then came the Etruscans, the superior race from northern Italy, probably of Asian extraction. They held sway between 616 and 578BC under three kings: Tarquinius Priscus, Servius Tullius, and Tarquinius Superbus. Historians once believed that the Servian Wall, an 11km (seven mile) defense still visible around present day Rome, dated from the time of Servius Tullius (c. 579–534BC). Now it is felt more likely that the original wall lies a long way beneath restoration work carried out much later.

In about 510BC Etruscan rule was overthrown, either through frustration among Rome's inhabitants at the despotism of the monarchy, or fury at the rape, by the son of Tarquinius Superbus, of a Roman woman who later committed suicide. One of the dead woman's relatives, Lucius Junius Brutus, is credited with the rebellion.

Above:

Forum

For centuries the Forum was the focus of political and commercial life in ancient Rome. It was an early civic center, equivalent to the Greek agora. Most of Rome's Forum was laid out in the first century BC but it was subsequently remodeled as each emperor tried to architecturally outdo his predecessor.

Next came the Roman Republic, a remarkable system of government, which would have been a credit to a far later civilization. It was led by two annually-elected consuls from the government, who had their powers both endorsed and curbed by a senate of elders with the power of veto. Re-election, at first prohibited, was later permitted after ten years had lapsed. No one was qualified for the role of consul until they had held a succession of junior posts in the government system. They could not be prosecuted for misdemeanors while they held high office, but would face the music when their term was up. In times of crisis there was provision for a dictator — a word we all know well today — to be picked for a limited six-month period.

The Senate was composed of the powerful patrician class. At first it was these elite few who had the benefit of a vote. The lower classes were plebeians although, after 367BC, they were by no means confined to their social order. In government they were represented by ten elected tribunes. Plebeians who made the grade and rivaled patricians in terms of wisdom and wealth simply crossed the class divide to become patrician.

This system of government gave the Roman Republic immense strength. However, the era was not without its difficulties. The fearsome Gauls sacked Rome in 390BC and there were successive conflicts with Carthage, the powerful North African trading base, in what were known as the Punic Wars. The most successful of the Punic leaders was Hannibal (c. 247–183BC) who daringly crossed the Alps into Italy with soldiers and war elephants in 218BC. Roman commanders, following their republican constitution to the letter,

Above:

Curia

The Curia, or senate house, that stands today in the Forum is a 1930s
reconstruction of the original. It overlooks the Via Sacra, or Sacred Way, the
Forum's central thoroughfare.

swapped roles every six months and became exposed by a lack of continuity.
Hannibal's run of triumphs was finally curtailed by the prodigiously talented
general Publius Cornelius Scipio (c. 236–183BC), who was granted overall
command at the age of 23 without having undergone the stipulated service in
public office. Carthaginian unrest continued to cause problems. Not until
146BC was Carthage brought to bay by the Romans. There were also spats
with the Greeks (or Macedonians), whose classical culture would eventually
be consumed by Rome.

These were golden days, with Rome benefiting from imported beliefs and
ideas. Until a Carthaginian ship was captured in the first Punic War there was
no Roman navy. The design was soon copied however, enabling the Romans
to put to sea, and with their rapidly developed navy the Romans were subsequently well equipped for future conquest and trade.

From the Greeks the Romans borrowed architectural style, prose, and
poetry — the essence of a classical culture. A further result of the Roman
Republic's expansionism was the influx of slaves, boosting the population of
Rome to about half a million in 100BC. Slavery was, of course, a way of life
with no moral questions asked.

However, the republic's days were numbered. There was a damaging split
between the senatorial class and the rest of society that slowly widened into a
fissure. Brothers Tiberius and Gaius Gracchus, tribunes determined to do
their best by the common people, were murdered at the behest of the Senate.

Meanwhile, the immensely powerful army increasingly found that it owed its allegiance to its commanders rather than the rulers of Rome. The fabric of the republic began unraveling when it was challenged by power-hungry generals like Cornelius Sulla (138–78BC) who stormed Rome, murdered numerous political rivals, and cowed the remainder into electing him dictator for a decade.

Although Sulla failed to last the ten year term — and even tried to repair the damage he had done to the Senate before he retired in 79BC — his actions weakened the system of government. Soon afterward there emerged three political giants. Gnaeus Pompeius (106–48BC), also known as Pompey the Great, Marcus Crassus (115–53BC), and Julius Caesar (100–44BC). The first two were involved in crushing the rebellion by the gladiator Spartacus in 71BC, although history tells that it was Crassus who did the work and Pompey who took the credit.

Nevertheless, the powerful trio agreed to join forces to look after one another's interests in various areas of Roman public life. The resulting First Triumvirate was moderately successful and brought a degree of stability to Roman government. However, it was not to last. By 54BC Crassus had been defeated and killed in battle at Parthia. Pompey, who had married Caesar's daughter to cement their alliance, found himself a widower and was increasingly drawn by the Senate, which was opposed to Caesar.

The latter spent years away campaigning in Gaul and beyond. When he finally returned to Italy in 49BC he found himself at war with Pompey, a fight ultimately won by Caesar. Pompey fled to Egypt where he was assassinated.

A similar fate was in store for Caesar, as the history books record. But his death did not occur until after a victorious return to Rome after which he pushed the Senate to make him dictator, first for one year, then ten years, and finally for life.

According to legend, Julius Caesar was the first baby to be born by caesarian section, an operation which allows babies to be born through the abdominal wall if they are unable to exit in the usual manner.

After distinguishing himself as a soldier, commander, and writer — following a conflict at Anatolia he wrote the much-quoted words *"veni, vidi, vici,"* which translates to "I came, I saw, I conquered" — Caesar sought absolute political power .

It was this tendency to tyranny that was to bring his eventual downfall. An increasing number of highly placed Roman people feared that he was unduly impressed and influenced by the Egyptian system of government in which the ruler was worshipped as a god. (Cleopatra, Queen of Egypt, had been his mistress.) Despite obvious abuses, the concept that the Roman people were sovereign — encapsulated in the phrase *Senatus Populusque Romanus* — was still dearly held.

Even his supporters were concerned at the threat he posed to the republic. His reforms, including a new, more logical calendar, extending Roman citizenship to conquered hordes and expanding the Senate, were laudable but insufficient to save him from plotters among rival senators. There was also gossip and mock horror about his sexual exploits, which involved both married women and men.

Thrice-married Caesar was killed in the Teatro di Pompeo on the Ides of March in 44BC. In the dramatization by William Shakespeare, Caesar's death is greeted with cries of "Liberty! Freedom! Tyranny is dead!" Yet academics are swift to point out that Sulla did as much damage to the republican system of government as ever Caesar did. Caesar was a brilliant strategist who inspired deep loyalty among his soldiers and as a ruler brought stability to the Mediterranean. He was also aware of the threat posed by human frailty, once observing, "History proves that by practicing cruelty you earn nothing but hatred. Nobody has ever achieved a lasting victory by such means except Sulla, and Sulla is not a man I propose to imitate." His judgement appears to have been fatally impaired in his final years.

But looking through the eyes of Caesar how did Rome appear in those distant times? He beheld the work of the consuls, proud of their heritage yet curbed by the moderation of the era — the excesses of the emperors were still to come. When he surveyed the Circus Maximus (Circo Massimo), laying in a valley between the Palatine and Aventine, he did not see the grassy stretch that appears to visitors today but ancient Rome's largest stadium, built in about the 4th century BC and a commanding 600m (2,000ft) long and 90m (300ft) wide. In Caesar's time it would have held some 250,000 spectators in the wooden grandstands, reveling in entertainments such as chariot racing, athletic contests, and wild animal fights. Executions, including crucifixions, were also staged here. The thrill for the audience lay not only in the spectacle of the blood sports but in betting on the outcome as gambling was a major preoccupation with Romans of the time. In the center of the circus, shaped as it was like a broad, prodding finger, there lay a barrier or spina along which seven egg-shaped objects were placed used for counting the laps in a race. Even the most experienced charioteer had to negotiate the sharp corners with care. It was here that Caesar had several of his key victories re-created, using prisoners of war as "extras."

Caesar died before the seven bronze dolphins were placed along the spina, and it was his successor Augustus who built the Imperial box under the Palatine and introduced an Egyptian obelisk dedicated to Ramses II to the arena, marking the conquest of that country. The stone needle — now 3,000 years old — stands in the Piazza del Popolo, one of 13 such obelisks that exist in Rome compared with just five left standing in Egypt.

The great fire of 64AD which destroyed much of Rome was thought to have started at the Circus Maximus. Afterward the arena was rebuilt under Emperor Trajan and remained in use until 549AD. In stark contrast to its previous incarnation it is now a haven of tranquility

Caesar would have had a choice of religions and, like other Roman citizens, could practice any without fear of reprisals. There was Judaism, Mithraism, and the worship of Isis, Osiris, and Atargatis among others. Although it was falling into disrepair, Caesar was surely inspired by the grandeur of the Etruscan Temple of Jupiter Capitolinus, built some five centuries before he

Above:
Markets of Trajan

Here is one of the earliest shopping complexes ever constructed. The markets of Trajan, built in the second century, contained 150 shops and offices. The items hawked there included spices from the Middle East as well as luxury goods imported from China along the Silk Road.

came to power. It measured about 71m (230ft) by 64m (210ft), the largest of its type known to have existed. Quite how the wooden structure, with its columns and terracotta decorations, would have appeared to Caesar's eye is difficult to tell. Scant traces of it remain but archaeologists have concluded it was similar in size to the Pantheon, Greek in appearance with six columns along its frontage, and contained a podium. Only its base remains today, in the Capitoline Museum.

Roman town planning was famous for its sewerage systems. The grandfather of all sewers was the Cloaca Maxima, built to help drain the Pontine marshes in the days of the Etruscan king Tarquinius Priscus, and broad enough to admit a wagon loaded with hay. Pliny the Elder, writing some seven centuries later, told how construction workers often chose suicide to escape the dreary labor — and how a scheme was found to eradicate the problem:

> "For this evil, however, the king devised a singular remedy, and one that has never been resorted to either before or since: for he ordered the bodies of all who had been thus guilty of self-destruction to be fastened to a cross and left there as a spectacle to their fellow citizens and a prey to birds and wild beasts."

The sewerage system was in operation in Caesar's time and remains so today.

In addition there were aqueducts providing the city with water and the first stone bridge built in Rome in 142BC was well used. The bridge — Ponte Rotto—finally fell down in 1598.

Above:

Roman Roads

Is there any more permanent reminder of Roman civilization than its roads?
Running straight as an arrow to a building standard that wouldn't be equaled for
centuries, Rome's roads took her legions to the extremities of the empire, and
brought back slaves and booty.

Caesar would certainly have traveled along the Appian Way (Via Appia
Antica) known in those days as *regina viarum*, the queen of roads. Here was
a thoroughfare begun as early as 312BC and built spectacularly straight. It
was ultimately extended to Brindisi, although not until 190BC. The significance of the road was such that, after the uprising led by Spartacus was
subdued in 71BC, 6,000 rebel slaves were crucified along the roadside by
way of a deterrent. This must have been a terrible panorama of suffering for
the many travelers who used the Appian Way, and a fearful reminder of
Rome's vengeance.

Yet brutality on this scale was not common during Caesar'a era. Most
inhabitants would remember the road at the time as being lined with new and
prestigious buildings, the ruins of which can still be seen today. Constructions
were brick built or featured concrete. It was during the reign of the Emperor
Augustus, Caesar's nephew and successor, that marble became construction
currency. Indeed, the emperor boasted that he found Rome in brick and left it
in marble. Other roads in existence in Caesar's day were the Via Flaminia, over
the Apennines, and the Via Aurelia, along the west coast.

The Temples of the Forum Boarium, fine examples of Roman culture
crossed with Greek, were about 150 years old when Caesar lived. One was
dedicated to Portunus, the god of rivers and ports, while the other was
devoted to Hercules. They appear today much as they did then, for the
buildings were adopted by Christians in the Middle Ages and were cherished
as churches.

Just completed was the Theater of Pompey, Rome's first permanent theater made of stone and concrete where Caesar would eventually meet his assassins.

The Roman Forum was a key feature in everyday life. Originally a marshy valley, marked only by an Iron Age cemetery it later became a produce market. For although the Romans were remembered best as soldiers they were from the earliest years children of the soil who, for numerous centuries, deemed farming every bit as important as conquest. Only after it was drained were buildings of consequence put up in the Forum. Today visitors see a modern reconstruction of the Curia, the chamber of the Roman Senate.

The Mamertine Prison, a dark, dank crypt into which criminals and enemies of the state were hurled to face starvation or strangulation, would have been one way for Caesar to dispense justice. It was here that Vercingetorix, leader of the rebel Gauls who were finally defeated by Caesar in 46BC met his death after being paraded as a trophy of victory through the streets of Rome.

Also in the Forum at the time of Caesar were the Basilica Aemilia, built in 179BC, a predecessor to the existing Temple of Saturn, the Rostra — remodeled by Caesar himself—the Temple of Castor and Pollux, and the Forum of Caesar, financed by the leader from his forays into Gaul.

Yet in and around the Forum much of what we see today would be unfamiliar to Caesar—the Colosseum, the Arch of Septimus Severus, the Column of Phocas, the Temple of Vesta, and the Temple of Venus and Rome, to name but a few.

And it is fair to say that some of these familiar historical monuments might never have been built had Caesar lived to be an old man. He had ambitious plans for Rome. The Basilica Julia, begun by Caesar in 54BC and completed after his death was only the start. The way Rome might have looked is a matter for the imagination.

His successor, his great nephew Octavius, instituted a far more modest building program — although it was nevertheless extensive. And before any such mundane tasks could be considered he had to negotiate the difficult job of securing power for himself.

On Caesar's death Mark Anthony, lover of Queen Cleopatra of Egypt, filled the void. Octavius was only 18 at the time and far less experienced in Roman politics. Biding his time, Octavius did not come into conflict with Mark Anthony until 31BC when he beat the old warhorse in a sea battle at Actium. Octavius became the Emperor Augustus and ruled for some 45 years over a largely peaceful domain.

Observers tell us that Augustus was handsome, even in his old age. He was known for being gentle, kindly, and wise, although he was equally capable of brutality and even stupidity. The people of Rome, however, had felt emotional and economic constraints during the previous years of unrest and political uncertainty. They were ready for some stability and this is just what Augustus, at the start of the Imperial Roman Empire, supplied. Under his stable influence the population of Rome exceeded one million and surpassed rivals Antioch and Alexandria in size and status. Some historians argue that

Rome deserved its title of *caput mundi* or "head of the world" for just a short spell coinciding with Augustan rule and went into its long decline following his death. Augustus was also smart enough to appear less the despot, more the benevolent people's choice, adopting the title *princeps* or first citizen rather than emperor. Edward Gibbon (1737–94), the author of *The History of the Decline and Fall of the Roman Empire*, said that Augustan rule was "an absolute monarchy disguised by the forms of a commonwealth."

Augustus was duly succeeded by Tiberius who was in power at the time Jesus was crucified in Roman-occupied Palestine. While Tiberius was underwhelming he was at least in command of all his faculties, which is more than can be said of Caligula, the next incumbent. It appears that a major illness just six months into his reign drove Caligula insane. He murdered or banished much of his family, had people tortured as entertainment during dinner and famously made his favorite horse a Roman consul. Unsurprisingly, he was assassinated by the powerful Praetorian Guard, the elite imperial soldiers.

The surprise success story of the era was 51-year-old Claudius, physically impeded and lacking character. The Praetorian Guard that proclaimed him Emperor upon the death of Caligula had to root him out from a hiding place in the Imperial Palace.

His wife Messalina was at first the power behind the throne, settling old scores and practicing various cruelties. Only when she staged a mock marriage to her lover in the center of Rome did Claudius bow to pressure and dispatch her, by execution. He went on to conquer much of Britain, despite the best efforts of native warriors Caratacus and Boudicca. Claudius' ability went largely unrecognized in his day. Only recently have historians appreciated his ability as an administrator.

The scales tipped again when Claudius died after being poisoned — probably by his second wife Agrippina. Her son, Nero, came to power at the tender age of 16. At first Nero had an able bank of advisors at his disposal and his reign was equable. But later, the darker side of his personality came to the fore. He had his mother, adoptive brother, and first wife killed, among others. While he provided sporting spectacles and grain for the masses, he was also responsible for beginning persecution of the infant Christian sect. Neither did he earn friends with his overt love of drama and music. However, he was also the victim of the terrible rumor, certainly untrue, that he started the fire of Rome which destroyed two thirds of the city in 64AD.

Ultimately, the Senate and the Praetorian Guards turned against him and Nero committed suicide.

The tussle that then took place for the crown of Rome was finally won by Vespasian, the first of the Flavian emperors.

History is rich with detail about the emperors of the Julio-Claudian dynasty — begun by Augustus and ending with Nero — and the subsequent Flavian emperors thanks to the copious writings of the observers of the era.

Famous among these are Tacitus, Livy, Virgil, Strabo, Ovid, Seneca, Pliny the Elder, Pliny the Younger, Plutarch, and Suetonius, all of whom were generous with their descriptions of Roman leaders, Roman exploits, and Rome

Above:
Baths of Caracalla
The communal baths built by the Emperor Caracalla (187–217 AD) — who
was assassinated in the year they were opened — were richly decorated
with mosaics, many of which have since been removed to museums. As
many as 1,500 bathers could indulge themselves at the baths, in a
succession of hot, warm, and cold pools.

herself. Indeed, Suetonius' *Lives of the Emperors* is something of an early gossip column, full of scurrilous tittle-tattle. However, in the absence of eminent writers there are fewer details known about subsequent generations of emperors. Those that are remembered at all are usually responsible for instigating a major architectural triumph that has survived the rigors of the passing years.

The words of the writers tell us much about life in ancient Rome and how it looked. Suetonius leaves us this description of Rome after Augustus:

"The whole space of the city he divided into wards and streets. He ordained that, as magistrates or aldermen yearly by lot should keep and govern the former so there should be masters or constables elected out of the commons of every street, to look unto the other. Against skarfires he devised night-watches and watchmen. To keep down inundations and deluges he enlarged and cleansed the channel of the river Tiber, which in times past was full of rammell and the ruins of houses, and so by that means narrow and choked."

That's in addition to the works left by the emperors themselves. Julius Caesar was a clever writer and it is through him that we know so much of the less eloquent races of the time, the Gauls and the Celts.

Above:

Coliseum

In ancient times gladiators formed part of the Etruscan funeral ceremony as a form of human sacrifice. Although Etruscan influence in Rome waned early on gladiatorial combat survived as a popular sport. After the Coliseum was inaugurated by the Emperor Titus in 80 AD there was a celebratory games which lasted for 100 days and nights and cost the lives of 5,000 animals.

Augustus was also in the habit of writing, below he relates his many architectural achievements in Rome, of which he was rightly proud.

"I built: the Curia and the Chalcidicum which adjoins it, the Temple of Apollo on the Palatine and its colonnades, the Temple of Divus Julius, the Lupercal, the Colonnade by the Circus Faminius (which I allowed to be called the Porticus Octavia, from the name of the Octavius who built an earlier colonnade on the same site), the imperial box in the Circus Maximus, the Temple of Jupiter Feretrius on the Capitol, and also that of Jupiter Tonans, the Temple of Quirinus, the Temples of Minerva and of Juno Regina and of Jupiter the Giver of Freedom on the Aventine, the Temple of the Lares on the summit of the Sacred Way, the Temple of the Penates on the Velia, the Temple of Juventas, the Temple of Magna Mater on the Palatine."

No mean epitaph. But he was not the only emperor with designs on Rome. No one can visit the city without feeling the potency of the Coliseum, begun during the reign of Vespasian, completed at the time of his first son Titus, and added to before the untimely death of his second son Domitian. It is not only the grand scale of the building that is so affecting — four stories high, stone built, and free-standing with room for 45,000 seated spectators and a further

5,000 "on the terraces" on a half acre site. It was solidly built, the Romans having learned bitter lessons about amphitheater construction. (In 27AD an estimated 50,000 people died when an amphitheater just outside the city collapsed.) Nevertheless, as a further safeguard there were 80 exits through which the amphitheater could be cleared in moments. Beneath its floor there was a maze of corridors and trap doors through which combatants were propelled into the ring. It was a distinguished building that symbolized grandeur and pride. Just what the designers and builders would have thought when, years later, the Coliseum was robbed of its stones for local building work is surely unprintable.

Still, it is the macabre history of the place that chills the bones even during a sticky Roman summer.

In the arena, gladiators — prisoners of war or slaves trained in combat — met with one another for a fight to the death. Men were pitted against comrades they had been eating and sleeping alongside for months and years beforehand. At the end, caked in sweat and grime, a gladiator often had to appeal to the crowd for his life. A thumbs up indicated survival, a thumbs down from the crowd meant death. When they were not compelled to kill one another gladiators had to face wild animals including lions and bears. This occurred until 523AD so the death toll must have been phenomenal. The Emperor Trajan once held a games lasting 117 days, during which 9,000 gladiators met their deaths. The bloodshed during combat was colossal. The crowd always bayed for more. After all, it was by hosting such grim spectacles that leaders hoped to win popularity among the people. Sometimes the amphitheater was flooded so that naval battles could be reconstructed for the benefit of the people.

The site was declared sacred in the Middle Ages to honor the Christians believed to have been martyred there. In fact, more recent evidence suggests that Christians were mostly killed in the imperial circuses. Yet the significance of the Coliseum is beyond question. Its solid splendor moved Lord Byron to write: "While stands the Coliseum, Rome shall stand; when falls the Coliseum, Rome shall fall; And when Rome falls — the world."

Today the amphitheater has renewed purpose. As the 20th century closed, the lighting of the Coliseum was changed from a mellow glow to bright white lights. The lights will change from white to gold when a convict is spared execution or if a country abandons the death penalty. Behind this laudable campaign is the Italian government — responding to a national distaste for the death penalty — the Vatican, Amnesty International, and the United Nations.

Parallels have been drawn by anti-death penalty protestors at the way Roman emperors deflected public criticism and increased their popularity with gladiatorial events and the way modern leaders exploit executions to their own ends during election campaigns. As a further postscript to the age of gladiators the sport of this kind of combat has once again become the vogue in Italy as a remedy for stress in the executive world without, of course, death or excessive injury.

The lust for blood was reflected in the way Rome was run, with murder and conspiracy rife among the upper echelons of society. Few of Rome's 78 emperors died as old men in their beds. Indeed, only a handful exceeded 20 years in power, the vast majority managing just a few years in the top job.

By the fourth century Rome was, architecturally speaking, at its classical zenith. Each emperor tried to outdo his predecessor and the city benefited greatly from this competitive spirit. Ammianus Marcellinus related how the city impressed the Emperor Constantine.

> "As the Emperor reviewed the vast city and its environs, spreading along the slopes, in the valleys and between the summits of the Seven Hills, he declared that the spectacle which first met his eyes surpassed everything he had yet beheld. Now his gaze rested on the Temple of Tarpeian Jupiter, now on baths so magnificent as to resemble entire provinces, now on the massive pile of the amphitheater, massively compact, or Tivoli stone, the summit of which seems scarcely accessible to the human eye, now on the Pantheon, rising like a fairy dome, and its sublime columns with their gently inclined staircases adorned with statues of departed emperors . . . When, however, he came to the Forum of Trajan, a structure unequalled by any other of its kind throughout the word, so exquisite, indeed that the gods themselves would find it hard to refuse their admiration, he stood as if in a trance, surveying with a dazed air the stupendous fabric which neither words can picture nor mortal ever again attempt to rear."

Alas, the empire was unraveling fast. Its borders were enormous and therefore indefensible. Byzantium — another seven hill city — had been the counterbalance in the East to Rome in the West. In 324 the Roman Emperor Constantine the Great, a man inspired by a vision of Christ's monogram in the sky, chose to make it the capital of his empire above Rome. He renamed it Constantinople and its political star rose to eclipse that of Rome.

People who had once haunted the borders of the empire — the Huns, Goths, and Vandals — could no longer be kept at bay. Rome's final emperor, Romulus Augustulus, was ousted by Odoacer the Goth in 475. The attacks were devastating, with much of Rome's small scale ancient finery looted.

Consequently, medieval Rome was smaller and less populous than neighboring cities — a shadow of its former self. The aqueducts were cut in the invasion of the fifth century AD and never repaired. This left the filthy Tiber as the main water source so disease was rife in the city.

Nature lent a hand in the destruction of the glorious buildings of ancient Rome — and so did the locals who carted off stones to be used in fortifications against the marauders of the day. Fortunately there were numerous ancient architectural treasures and comparatively few inhabitants in the sixth, seventh, and eighth centuries when the population fell to just 20,000.

Testimony to this comes from John Raymond, a traveler of the 17th century, who still found that: "A man may spend many months at Rome and yet have something of note to see every day."

Above:

Trastavere

Rome spreads before you when you stand in Trastavere, on the left bank of the Tiber. Indeed, the very name Trastevere is drawn from the words trans Tiberium, across the Tiber. Although divided from the city by the river it was thought sufficiently important to warrant the protection of the Aurelian Wall.

Still, Rome was contriving a new and enduring role — as head of the Christian church.

Although based in the East the burgeoning Christian movement could hardly neglect the role of St. Peter, the man to whom Christ left the leadership of the church, who was martyred in Rome in 63AD when he was crucified upside down. Likewise Paul was sent to Rome for trial and was martyred there. In laying claim to two of the most fundamental saints, Rome was assuring itself of a future.

There was already a small Christian brigade — mostly slaves and poor people — in Rome, even before the arrival of Peter and Paul. Word was presumably carried by traders or merchants and the proof of it is in the catacombs on the outskirts of Rome where early Christians were buried. The walls are covered with frescoes and the texts of tombstones which bear witness to the early sufferings of the Christians who Nero persecuted in a bid to divert attention from his own failings.

The early popes were keenly evangelist. Indeed, they insisted that other churches followed their example. This resulted in canon law and layers of bureaucracy that would typify the church for centuries to come. Meanwhile, the lifestyle of the popes often did not bear scrutiny.

There were some worthy popes, including St. Leo I (reigned 440–61) who negotiated with Attila the Hun and the marauding Vandals to prevent an invasion of Rome. Astonishingly, 96 of his sermons and 143 letters have been preserved. St. Gregory (reigned 590–604) was a trained lawyer, an effective

Above:
Garden of Paradise

Mosaics like these, depicting the Virgin and Child in the Garden of Paradise
with Pope Pascal I, are often found in Rome's numerous churches.

missionary, and a dynamic leader of the Church. He is known as the father of
the medieval papacy.

St. Gelasius I, (reigned 492–96), is likewise remembered for his collection
of legal documents, which helped shape the papacy of the Middle Ages. Yet
the popes, who were saviors of Rome in those dark days, were occasionally
compelled to move out of Rome — to Ravenna on the coast or to Avignon in
France — when the city became downright dangerous.

From the early Middle Ages the popes were becoming an increasing
political force. With one eye on the Byzantine empire in the East, St. Leo III
(reigned 795–816) crowned Charlemagne as head of what was to become the
Holy Roman Empire on Christmas Day in 800, reinstating the Roman Empire
at least in name. It gave the papacy muscle and put the popes in the midst of
the European supremacy struggle, with power to make or break emperors.

The evolving papacy took on some questionable mantles. In 1231 Pope
Gregory IX (who was elected pope in 1227 at the age of 86 and reigned for 14
years) instituted the Inquisition or Holy Office to combat the growing number
of heretics in the Christian world.

By this method the life of those in southern Europe was controlled by the
popes for 400 years. The Inquisition is best remembered for its cruelty and
ruthlessness illustrated by the widespread use of torture to elicit confessions.

The self-educated son of an innkeeper, Cola di Rienzo (1313–54) tapped
popular support to win the leadership of Rome while the popes ruled from

Avignon in France. Not only was there lawlessness and decay but a spate of natural disasters including two earthquakes and the plague, which brought Rome to ruin. Cola trained in the law and read Roman classics that inspired him to visions of greatness for the city. On Whit Sunday in 1347 he summoned mercenaries to help him depose the civic government and declared himself Tribune of Rome, joint ruler alongside the absent pope. He was forced to flee when the pope's representatives moved against him and, when he returned to Rome six years later, was killed by a mob. Although he is thought to have been bordering on madness, the power of his oratory was sufficient to bring Petrarch to Rome in anticipation of a Roman revival. Cola's dreams of a united Italy with Rome as its heart took a further five centuries to materialize.

By the late 15th century the papacy was sunk into iniquity. Pope Sixtus IV (1414–85) — remembered primarily as the man who began the Sistine Chapel — was keen to see the "family firm" get ahead, particularly in its long-running rivalry with the Medicis of Florence. No fewer than seven of his nephews were made cardinals. Of him, Machiavelli wrote: "He was the first who began to show how far a pope might go, and how much which was previously regarded as sinful loses its iniquity when committed by a pontiff."

Alexander VI (1431–1503) had at least four children before becoming pope — and fathered more after reaching high office. A member of the powerful Borgian family, he was notorious for his immorality, nepotism, and extravagance. "The pope has no care for aught but exalting his children by hook or by crook," wrote one observer at the time.

And when Pope Leo X (1475–1521) got the job in 1513 he said to his brother: "God has given us the papacy. Let us enjoy it." He was as good as his word and in throwing lavish dinner parties, sponsoring theater, music, and hunting, he propelled the papacy into terrible debt.

However, the position of pope was highly sought after and there was much scheming between the major families and emperors of the time to place friends or relations in it. These kind of excesses fueled the Reformation, beginning in Germany with the remonstrations of Martin Luther in 1521.

Proof of the papal pre-eminence is all about Rome in the shape of the splendid churches built from the 4th century to the 15th and beyond. There's the magnificent St. Peter's, at 137m (450ft) the tallest dome in the world. It's not the original of course. That was built in 326AD on the orders of the Emperor Constantine above the grave of St. Peter. The masonry crumbled and was finally demolished for the "new" St. Peter's. Building began in 1506. Controversially, some of the costs of construction were covered through the sale of indulgences, by which sins were forgiven in exchange for cash. This was one of the very practices about which Luther raged.

It took 120 years to complete St. Peter's under 13 chief architects, including Raphael and Michelangelo. The main structure is 187m (613ft) long and stands 20m (67ft) higher than St. Paul's in London and 45m (148ft) higher than the dome of America's Capitol. It was finally consecrated in 1626 by Pope Urban VIII, a scholarly fellow who nevertheless deemed it necessary to condemn the science of Galileo through the Inquisition.

The famous mosaics of the Santa Maria Maggiore date from the fifth century. By legend, Pope Liberius was told in a dream by the Virgin Mary to build a church on the spot where he found snow. Apparently he found it on the Esquiline in Rome even though it was an August morning and set about building the Santa Maria Maggiore. The church has been added to over the years in splendid style.

Rome was further enhanced when it finally became infected by the revolution in art, design, and philosophy that was unfolding in Tuscany. It is an era known as the Renaissance.

To define the Renaissance, its exact beginnings and its end, is an impossible task. In essence, it began when eminent folk such as Petrarch pondered the glories of ancient Rome and sought to imitate its success in arts and literature. The period is associated with tolerance, humanism, creativity, culture, and Italy. Interestingly, the term "Renaissance" — meaning re-birth — was not coined until the middle of the 19th century and since then there have been a multitude of arguments to say that it is impractical to address one period in history in such a simplistic way.

The first artistic works regarded as Renaissance to appear in Rome were the central bronze doors of St. Peter's. There followed the Villa Farnesina and the Palazzo Farnese as well as churches including Santa Maria del Popolo, Santa Maria della Pace, and the Sistine Chapel. Given that most of the patrons were from religious orders or of pious intent, Renaissance art was overwhelmed with Christian imagery.

The richness of artistic life in Rome at the time was awesome. A trip around the Vatican museums will give the visitor some inkling of the vast creative outpouring. Julius II (1443–1513), a man of immense personal vanity, was pope and sought to re-build Rome in the manner of his namesake Julius Caesar. Michelangelo (1475–1564) was in competition with Raphael (1483–1520) for papal commissions and the bitterness of the rivalry between them is revealed in a letter sent by Michelangelo to a cardinal in 1542. "All the bad blood between Pope Julius and me was due to envy on the part of Bramante and Raphael of Urbino . . . They wanted to ruin me, and Raphael had good reason, for everything he knew about art came from me."

Raphael seemed to have greater popularity in his short lifetime than Michelangelo — perhaps in part because of the latter's difficult nature. Only after both were dead and buried were they deemed equally exceptional.

First and foremost a sculptor, Buonarroti Michelangelo was also a painter, architect, and poet. He was born to a well-to-do family in Florence and, although his family at first resisted his artistic ambitions, he was made a pupil to the artist Domenico Ghirlandaio (1449–94) by his father. However, he later claimed to his biographer, with some credence, that his sculpting skills were largely self-taught.

Michelangelo paid several extended visits to Rome, once to escape feuding in Florence, secondly at the invitation of Pope Julius II in March 1505 to work on the latter's tomb. This became a major project for the artist and brought forth some grand plans. Economies forced the scheme to be scaled down — he

Above:

St. Peter's

Numerous architects and artists were involved in the building of the new St. Peter's (San Pietro) which took 123 years to complete. In essence the floor is Bramante's, the dome belongs to Michelangelo, the façade is the work of Carlo Maderno (1556–1629) and the oval colonnade which lies before the Basilica reveals the genius of Bernini (1598–1680).

called it "the tragedy of the tomb" — and eventually it was completed by Michelangelo's pupils. But it does feature upon the tomb his Moses, an extraordinary and perceptive sculpture.

In 1534 he settled forever in Rome and could not be lured back to his native Florence, despite every effort made by the ruling Cosimo I.

His most celebrated link with Rome is the decorative frescoes that adorn the ceiling of the Sistine Chapel. It was a prospect that first appalled him then intrigued him. He undertook the job on the basis that he worked alone and unobserved. In effect he reproduced the history of the Christian world in picture form, a passionate and powerful interpretation. These frescoes, and those on the walls of another Vatican chapel, the Cappella Paolina, make Michelangelo loom large to the visitor in Rome, even today.

Michelangelo is often called the father of the artistic style known as Mannerism and also Baroque. His works — often but not exclusively on a Christian theme — were intense and emotional. During his lifetime he became known as "the divine Michelangelo," yet talented though he was, his ideas were frequently more excessive than even his endeavor could achieve. Shortly before his death he burned many of his draft sketches so no one would realize he had ever fallen short of his own expectation.

When Raphael died on Good Friday in 1520 at the age of 37, a productive and inspired life was brought to a close. Raphael was born in Urbino, the son of an artist who worked in Mantua. As a youth he was a pupil of the artist Perugino who pioneered the use of oils. His work matured after visits to

Above:
Interior of St. Peter's

The inside of St. Peter's is incredibly opulent — as befits the most important venue for the Catholic Church. In the foreground of this picture is the intricate canopy of the Papal Altar. The gilded bronze roof is held up on spiral columns measuring 20m (66ft) high and was designed by Bernine. It is said to cover the spot where St. Peter's body is buried.

Florence and ultimately to Rome, where he was summoned by Pope Julius II to decorate a suite of rooms in the Vatican.

The frescoes, along with the designs for two tapestries illustrating the lives of St. Peter and St. Paul, are perhaps his most enduring creations. The content of his work reveals the influence of classical décor, particularly from the palace of Nero, which was being excavated during his lifetime.

Rahael did much work in Rome for private patrons, including the frescoes of the chapels at Santa Maria della Pace and Santa Maria del Popolo. His grace and harmony on canvas and in altar pieces were to influence succeeding generations of artists.

Donato Bramante (c. 1444–1514) was a painter turned architect whose influence on the Renaissance was equally as profound as that of Michelangelo or Raphael. He was born near Raphael's home town of Urbino and worked in Milan before moving to Rome in 1499. Favored by the extravagant Pope Julius II, Bramante set about changing the face of Rome and earned himself the nick-name "Ruinante." For it was the ruins of classical Rome that inspired him. His first major work in Rome was the Tempietto of San Pietro in Montorio — marking the spot where St. Peter was believed to have died — which was remarkably similar in appearance to the Roman Temple of the Sibyl at Tivoli.

It was Bramante who was behind the plans for the rebuilding of St. Peter's in Rome in the Greek-cross design, as well as a spacious addition to the Vatican Palace. His plans were both innovative and practical — he invented techniques and materials that facilitated major economies in the execution of his grand designs.

The last of many sackings of Rome came in 1527. France had invaded the Italian peninsula and Italy became the battlefield for the vying political powers of Europe. When Pope Clement VII backed the French against the Holy Roman Emperor, Charles V, Rome became a target. It was a barbarous affair with some 20,000 troops, German and Spanish, pouring into the city. The pope was forced to seek refuge in the Castel Sant'Angelo, a fortified building constructed on the Emperor Hadrian's tomb. The fast-talking, loose-living goldsmith Cellini later claimed to have been to pope's main defender, killing many with a new-found skill in marksmanship. According to Cellini: "(The Pope) gave me his blessing and forgave me all the deaths I had ever caused and all that I ever would cause in the service of the Apostolic Church."

Although the city did stage a remarkable recovery later, it lay in ruins following the invasion and it was nearly a year before normal life could be resumed. Some historians declare this violence and destruction marked the end of the Renaissance, although others say the correct date was the death of Michelangelo.

When Benvenuto Cellini (1500–71) penned his autobiography he took enormous satisfaction in shaping his life and exploits into a marvelous and compelling drama with himself center stage. Doubtless there was plenty of embellishment and exaggeration from this somewhat inflated ego, yet his words have left us a superb insight into life in Rome and elsewhere during the Renaissance. Indeed, he was a colorful character. Despite his prodigious talent as a goldsmith he was thrown out of Florence, his birthplace, as a punishment for his constant brawling. Afterward he moved to Rome, where he became a pupil of Michelangelo for a spell. He lived there between 1519 and 1540 and was, he claimed, a principal defender of the city during the sack of 1527. He then spent five years in France before finally returning to Florence, where he died.

Few pieces of his work are known to have survived — two seals, three medals, seven coins, seven sculptures, and the incomparable gold salt cellar crafted for Francis I of France (1494–1547).

After the sacking, Rome received the benefits of Baroque, another epoch making era in art. However, with the enthusiasm for Baroque architecture, much of the Gothic and Romanesque features of the city were rubbed out. Baroque is not to everybody's taste. The Italian writer Luigi Barzini said it was a metaphor "to describe anything pointlessly complicated, otiose, capricious, and eccentric."

As if to confirm its international stature Rome became the city on every gentleman's tour itinerary in the late 18th century. The poet Lord Byron was among them. So moved was he by the place that he exclaimed: "Oh Rome! My country! City of the soul!" German poet and scholar Johanne Wolfgang von Goethe was likewise enthused and in awe. "Rome is a world, and it would take years to become a true citizen of it. How lucky those travelers are who take one look and leave."

Short, stout, and strutting, Edward Gibbon (1737–94) cut a comical figure in 18th century Britain. Yet his work remains widely read today, a tribute to its quality and clarity. In fact, Gibbon hardly attended school as a boy due to sickness. After a spell at Oxford and in the Hampshire militia he devoted some time to touring Europe:

"It was at Rome, on the fifteenth of October 1764, as I sat musing amidst the ruins of the Capitol, while the barefoot friars were singing vespers in the Temple of Jupiter, that the idea of writing the decline and fall of the city first started to my mind."

The first volume of *Decline and Fall* appeared in 1776 and was followed five years later by a further two. The final three volumes were published in 1788.

In 1832 Mariana Starke reported in her *Traveller's Guide*: "At Rome . . . every person may find amusement: for whether it be our wish to dive deep into classical knowledge, whether arts and sciences be our pursuit, or whether we merely seek for new ideas and new objects, the end cannot fail to be obtained in this most interesting of cities, where every stone is an historian."

Following the Renaissance and Baroque periods Rome had to work hard to find a place in the hierarchy of Europe and the world. Italy at the time was not a unified country, rather a series of states and the principal influence in the region between the 16th and 18th centuries was Spain. Austria's star rose in the region for a while until the French Revolutionary armies arrived under the command of Napoleon and installed Napoleon's son as "Roi de Rome." For the first time the Italian states were as one and the seeds of nationalism were sown. Austrian rule was restored after the fall of Napoleon with the popes holding sway in Rome — but only until the likes of Garibaldi, Victor Emmanuel, and Cavour won the fight for independence. Garibaldi led the defense of a newly declared Roman Republic, following the ousting of a pope, against the French in 1848, becoming one of the heroic failures of those turbulent times.

The Kingdom of Italy was finally proclaimed in 1861. Five years later Venice was annexed on the infant Italy's behalf, and by 1870 the Vatican states had joined the fold. The popes had maintained their independence with the support of French troops, but when these were withdrawn the Italian army moved in. As a protest against the loss of his territories the pope retreated behind the walls of the Vatican. The era is known as the Risorgimento, which translates to resurgence. In 1870, too, Rome became the capital of the new Italy and this position entailed the construction of many new government buildings and other public offices that give Rome its wealth of 19th century facades.

Above:

Trevi Fountain

Work began on the Trevi Fountain in 1732 — and lasted for 30 years. Nicholas
Salvi is responsible for the design, which features Neptune, god of the sea,
with Tritons to each side. It is on the site of one of the early aqueducts
built in about 19BC.

Italy had been an independent state for just 50 years when Benito
Mussolini (1883–1945) led the rise of Fascism which so affected — or afflict-
ed — the nation and its people. The son of a blacksmith, Mussolini was a
veteran of the World War I, serving in the Italian trenches which, according
to historian A.J.P. Taylor, were the worst in Europe. First drawn to socialism,
Mussolini began his own political party, with ex-servicemen acting as his
ground force. The "Black Shirts," as they were known, paved the way to
power for Mussolini with their "March on Rome" in 1922. This show of
strength was enough to prompt an invitation to Mussolini to become prime
minister, a position he held for three years until he formed a one party state
with himself as leader. The name he adopted for himself was "Duce" or leader,
and the party symbol became the fasces, borrowed from ancient Rome when
Italians last been dominant on the world stage.

Ultimately, Mussolini lost power in Italy, was captured by Italian partisans,
and shot. His body, along with that of his faithful mistress Clara Petacci, was
strung up by the ankles in Milan to be stoned by an angry mob.

Rome's University City was also built in Mussolini's time, completed in
1935 after being three years under construction. The main railway station, the
Stazione di Termini, was opened in December 1950, ten years prior to the

Above:

Benito Mussolini

Benito Mussolini, like his co-fascist Adolf Hitler, had powers of rhetoric that
kept crowds agog for hours. Short of stature, he often positioned himself well
above the crowd to increase the sense of grandeur.

Stadio Flaminio and the Palazzo dello Sport, the additions to Rome made for
the Olympic Games. Sprawling suburbs have spread like a rash around
Rome since the war. However, one of the greatest changes in Rome this
century is the number of bridges spanning the Tiber. Where once there were
just five crossing points there are today 21 bridges, the latest being Ponte
Flaminio built in 1951.

Rome has found a new role in Italy in the last quarter of the 20th century,
as the home of a flourishing film industry. Fellini, Zeffirelli, and *La Dolce Vita*
are cult bywords among movie-goers. But despite the reviving of Rome's great
creative spirit, the city has been beset by problems and tragedy. Among the
bleakest of post-war memories are of violent student riots in the sixties and the
kidnapping and murder of former Prime Minister Aldo Moro in 1978 by
anarchic Brigate Rosse (Red Brigade) terrorists. He was held captive for 78
days and his body was found in a car boot parked in Via Caetani, midway
between the Christian Democrat headquarters and that of the Communists.
The antics of the B.R. and other terrorist groups had the years between 1973
and 1980 dubbed *Anni di Piombo* or "Years of the Bullet."

When is it best to see Rome? Avoid the August heat and January's chill.
Consider carefully the hassle factor of Rome's traffic-bound streets and the

thronging tourists eager to drink in the famous sights. As the French novelist Henri Stendhal (1783–1842) pointed out: "If the foreigner who enters St. Peter's tries to see everything, he will develop a furious headache and presently satiety and pain will render him incapable of any pleasure." Perhaps it is best to get the first notion of St. Peter's from a distance, standing atop one of Rome's hills.

If the citizens of Rome today are gruff to the point of rudeness it's because their city is choked with cars and packed with tourists. If that wasn't enough to contend with they are frequently insulted by other Italians who believe them profligate and lazy. The cynical claim that if you follow the old adage coined by St. Ambrose (340–390) — if you are at Rome live in the Roman style — then you would have plenty to eat and little to do.

Roman Catholicism is by no means the exclusive religion of the city. There's a mosque, synagogues, Protestant churches, and even a branch of the Salvation Army. But it is Catholicism that lured an estimated 30 million pilgrims to Rome in the Holy Year 2000 — an echo of the first Holy or Jubilee year proclaimed in 1300 by Pope Boniface VIII (1235–1303) and witnessed by Dante among others — which continued to renew the vibrancy of this city of classics and culture.

Rome's population now stands at about 3.5 million. Ten times that number were expected to visit the capital during the Millennium Jubilee of 2000 — as many as 200,000 people every day. The new century has inspired the building of several road links, a new stretch of Metro, and 15 new churches in Rome's suburbs.

Rome's traffic was already gridlocked, even before pilgrims for the Jubilee descended. At the end of 1999 the transport unions inflamed an already precarious situation by going on strike. However, union leader Pietro Larizza observed, "We're discovering that there's no need for strikes to paralyze Rome's transport system." The city council defended its position robustly. "Tourists like chaos," insisted one spokesman. "Take the Swiss for example. They always complain that their cities are like morgues and they like a bit of chaos when they come to Rome." Chaos is certainly never far away, and the anarchy of Roman traffic is legendary. Pedestrian tourists are issued with specific instructions about crossing the roads, as cars will often seem to be veering straight for them, even at a red light.

Attempts to improve car parking in the city have also been fraught with difficulties. The Vatican's plan for a multi-storey car park was delayed by the discovery of hitherto unknown ruins. The archaeological significance of the area was considered so great that it threatened the building of the planned ramp into the car park. Stumbling across supremely important sites like this is an occupational hazard for Rome's builders who are well used to the ensuing delays and dilemmas about future construction.

Despite appearances, not everything about the city is sublime. Its population has suffered mightily with an invasion of an Asian mosquito, the bite of which causes painful boils. The tiger mosquito, named for the stripes on its legs, was introduced to the outskirts of Rome in a consignment of second-hand tires and thrived thanks to the watering trays beneath geraniums on the city's window sills. Following a major de-infestation program, new legislation was introduced which meant that anyone found keeping stagnant water could be fined. Crime is also a problem in Rome as in every great city. Pickpockets — increasingly made up of gangs of small children — mark out tourists on public transport and in the city center; handbag thieves often operate from the back of motor scooters.

The eternal city is as eternally youthful: the young meet in the Piazza di Spagna as they have done for generations. True, the McDonalds here has become a draw but it has merely replaced the traditional eating houses where generations of European adolescents congregated. The Piazza was once referred to as the "English Ghetto" because of the number of English who stayed there as part of their Grand Tour. The influence of the English is still present today, with afternoon tea available at Babington's. For a more Italian experience Rome has plentiful cafés and restaurants to tempt the palette. Those with a sweet tooth should head for Caffe Giolitti to try its famous ice creams, while Caffe Greco is a shrine to artists and the literati, and a mecca for their aspirants.

Shopping in Rome can be an expensive pleasure to take. There are just a small handful of department stores and large suburban shopping malls, while the majority of stores are specific to a particular business. The Via Condotti is famous for its exclusive designer stores, where the tourist can enjoy some high-class window shopping, if nothing else.

With sporting activities, as with others in Rome, being seen can be more important than the activity itself. Thus hordes of well-heeled joggers can be seen dashing through the grounds of the Villa Pamphilj. More serious forms of sport are served by the stadium built for the 1960 Rome Olympics. Those who like their pleasures at a faster pace, though, need only step into a car and take a drive through Rome's streets.

Many visitors to Rome are struck by the breezy, even cavalier way Romans seem to live with their ancient surroundings; yet the Rome of today lives in two worlds: the impossibly old and the impossible new, each struggling for attention. Parallel to this is the struggle to accommodate a living, working city alongside a spiraling tourist trade. Rome has recently started to make many long overdue civic changes; it looks forward to further improvements that make that double life easier — a battle less likely to be lost by either side.

Right:

Arch of Titus

Built in 81AD, the magnificent Arco di Tito (Arch of Titus) commemorates the defeat of the Jewish rebellion in Jerusalem by the Emperor Titus (reigned 79-81AD), who is depicted victorious on his chariot. It stands on the fringes of the Forum, its inner walls bearing the scars of generations of cart wheels that entered the market place through the grandly worked arch.

Above:
Art for Sale
With so much beauty all around, Rome has always been a magnet for artists. These paintings are for sale in the
Piazza Navona, where they are guaranteed an audience of passing tourists.

Above:

Antique Market

Amongst the assembled junk of this flea market, or *mercato delle pulci*, you might just find an antique or two. The real appeal of such markets, however, is to the seasoned bargain hunter, who can haggle over second-hand clothing, furniture, paintings, and music: a Sunday morning institution.

Above:

Arch of Constantine

Dedicated in 315AD, three years after Constantine triumphed over rival Maxentius, the arch was a rebuild of one built by Trajan (reigned 98–117AD) and features reliefs of the earlier emperor's victories over the Dacians.

Right:

Aurelian Walls

As Rome's power declined there was a need for bigger, better defences than ever before. Emperor Aurelian (reigned 270–275AD) responded with a 20km (13 mile) wall standing some 7m (21ft) high, encircling the city and its seven hills. It had 18 fortified gates like this one, most of which are still in use.

Above:

Basilica of Constantine

The arches are about all that remain of the Basilica of Constantine in the Forum. Yet they alone are sufficient to suggest the immense grandeur of the place in its heyday during the fourth century. At that time it featured twisted columns and gilt bronze tiles reflecting in shiny marble floors, built to honor the Rome's first Christian emperor.

Above:

Bagpipe Musicians

The bagpipes are an ancient instrument, and part of global musical tradition. Although they are commonly associated with Scotland, they are no less important to the folk music of Italy. Here in the Piazza Navona, these traditionally dressed musicians keep a crowd enthralled with the eerie sounds of the bagpipes.

Above:
Caffè Greco

The Caffè Greco, founded in 1760, has known some famous customers in its time. Among the illustrious clientele of times gone by are Casanova, Goethe, Wagner, Baudelaire, Shelley, and Byron. Today tourists head for the sofas while locals tend to mingle in the foyer.

Right:
Casino del Bel Respiro

The Casino del Bel Respiro stands in the grounds of Villa Doria Pamphilj, today Rome's largest public park. Built by the sculptor Algardi, the 17th century home was named after the clean air of its environs. Since then it has been turned to various uses, but stands testament to the building zeal of that age.

Above:

Campo de'Fiori

In the Campo de'Fiori food, flowers, and other goods are for sale. Surrounding streets once housed the craftsmen
of the medieval period. Keys (*chiavi*) were available in the Via dei Chiavari, chairs (*sedie*) were sold down
Via dei Sederari, while jacket (*guibbotti*) makers gathered in Via dei Giubbonari.

Right:

Campo de'Fiori

Restaurants in the vicinity of Campo de'Fiori buy their produce from the fascinating open air market. Prices
are high but the atmosphere is buzzing. Get there early (it opens at 6am) because by lunchtime stallholders
are packing up and heading for much-needed refreshment in the surrounding streets.

Above:
Campidoglio
The Campidoglio, Rome's civic center designed by Michelangelo, summons up the spirit of the city in one building. Its sun-softened brickwork peppered with pleasing fripperies has a sense of balance and beauty that typifies the architect's work. Most of the buildings today are devoted to the exhibits of the Capitoline museums, although the mayor's office still occupies part of the complex.

Left:
Café in the Piazza Navona
In a city that takes its social duties seriously, a Rome without cafés is unimaginable. Roman cafés are the perfect pitstop, whether for a bite to eat, a pause for people-watching, or just a refreshing drink. Here tourists pass an evening at Caffè Bernini in the Piazza Navona.

Above:

Capitoline Museum

Marvelous frescoes cover the walls of the "Hall of Captains" in the Palazzo dei Conservatori of the Capitoline
Museum, which was once the preserve of city magistrates. Built in the mid-16th century the Palazzo
is now predominantly given over to art and sculpture.

Right:

Carabinierei

Italy's law enforcers include Carabinieri, the military police who wear dark blue uniforms with a red stripe, and la
Polizia, a civil force clad in light blue trousers with white helmets.

Above:

Church of San Gregoria Magno

The present façade of the San Gregoria Magno on the Celian Hill in Rome is a product of the work carried out by Giovanni Battista Soria from 1629. But the site was religiously significant for centuries before that, for it was here that St. Gregory the Great lived and from here St. Augustine was dispatched to convert England to Christianity.

Right:

Church of Gesu

Gesu, completed in 1584, was the first Jesuit church built in Rome. While Jesuits are best remembered as missionaries and teachers in far flung corners of the world it was they who led the Catholic backlash against the Reformation. The décor of the church is rich in adoration of the faith and is designed to encourage the Catholic worshipper and disparage the newly emerging Protestant faith.

Above:

Church of San Rocco

A beacon of compassion, San Rocco was a church better known as a hospital, specializing in helping poor or unmarried mothers to give birth. Mothers who insisted on secrecy were allowed to wear a veil in labor and their unwanted babies were sent to a local orphanage. The hospital wing was finally demolished in Mussolini's time as it stood atop Augustus' Mausoleum, but the church was left intact.

Right:

Church of Sant' Ignazio di Loyola

Built in 1626 to honor St. Ignatius, the founder of the Society of Jesus, or the Jesuits as they became known. Above the nave and the apse (pictured) the ceiling appears to extend into a cupola. In fact one was planned but never built. Decorators used perspective to create the illusion internally.

Above:

Church of Santa Maria Maggiore

Inside this church lies Pope Sixtus V (reigned 1585–90) in a dedicated chapel. But the basilica is more famous for its mosaics which were installed between the fifth and 14th centuries. Look up to see the splendidly gilded ceiling, which is said to include gold brought back by Christopher Columbus from the New World.

Right:

Church of Trinita dei Monti

The bell towers of Trinita dei Monti, the French church founded in 1495, loom above the Spanish Steps. The Steps are famous for the azaleas that bloom in containers from top to bottom.

Overleaf:

Circus Maximus

The Temple of Mithras under the Circus Maximus.

Above:

Coliseum

Pristine carriages are now a familiar sight around Rome's Coliseum where once chariots would have raced. A wall mounted memorial recalls the plight of the Christians who were persecuted to various degrees in ancient Rome. In fact, recent evidence has most of the Christian deaths taking place in the Imperial Circuses. It was gladiators that were killed in abundance here.

Right and Overleaf:

Coliseum

An international landmark, its lights have been modified to make the Coliseum a powerful protest against capital punishment. The illuminations will change from white to gold whenever a prisoner sentenced to death is spared or if the death penalty is abandoned in any of the numerous countries of the world where it is still common practice. Originally the stands were covered with an adjustable canvas awning to keep the baying crowds in comfort.

Above:

Fontana della Barcaccia

At the foot of the Spanish Steps lies the Fontana della Barcaccia, another fountain commissioned by Pope Urban VIII and probably designed by Bermini. If not, it was Bermini's father Pietro who drew up a leaky boat lying half submerged in the collection pool. Bees from the Barberini coat of arms feature on the stonework.

Right:

Fontana delle Api

Designed by Bernini, the Fontana delle Api, or Bee Fountain, is unobtrusively placed in the corner of Piazza Barberini. It was made by way of tribute to the Barberini family in 1644, the family symbol being a bee. Its primary purpose was to provide refreshment for the city's public and their animals.

Above:

Forum

The Arch of Septimus Severus, standing in the Forum, bears the date 203AD. It marks his achievements, yet it also bears witness to family tragedy. Following the death of Severus, his two sons fell out and one, Caracalla, murdered the other, Geta. The victim's name was removed from the arch, although traces of it remain visible.

Right:

Forum

Once the Roman Forum was the heart of the city — the central site for spiritual, commercial, and social activity. Today it appears as randomly placed rubble. That the ancient treasures survived at all when Rome fell after the end of imperial rule is a miracle. From the fifth century builders raided the area for stonework.

Previous page:

Forum

Three Corinthian columns dating from the reign of Tiberius (reigned 14–37AD) are about all that remain of the Temple of Castor and Pollux.

Above:

Forum: Temple of Antonius and Faustina

One of the Forum's best-preserved attractions, the Temple of Antonius and Faustina was begun in 141AD by Senate decree, on the death of Faustina.

Right:

Forum

Julius Caesar planned and partially built this forum, before forums became the fashion. To finance it he used wealth plundered from Gaul. In it originally there was a Temple and statues of Casesar, Cleopatra, and Venus. Damaged by fire in 80AD, Domitian and Trajan made additions, including a heated public lavatory.

Above:

Garibaldi Monument

Giuseppe Garibaldi, the active arch-nationalist, is a hero in Italy. The monument on Janiculum unveiled in 1895 shows the great man astride his steed. Around its base are scenes from the battle with the French that took place on Janiculum in 1849 when Italian soldiers held off superior numbers of the enemy for weeks until they were forced to flee.

Above:

Janiculuum Hill

Treasures on the Janiculum Hill include the Garibaldi Monument, Villa Farnesina, with its famous Renaissance frescoes, the Galleria Nazionale d'Arte Antica, the city's Botanical Gardens, Bramante's Tempietto, or round chapel, and the marvelous waterfeatures at Fontana Paola. It was from Janiculum in 1849 that Garibaldi repelled the French who threatened the unification of Italy.

Above:

Pope John Paul II

Pope John Paul II greets a delighted crowd on a tour through the streets of Rome. For many people who come to Rome a chance like this to see the Pope is a once-in-a-lifetime opportunity.

Previous page:

Mausoleum of Augustus

Inspired by the Mausoleum of Alexander, which the Octavian had seen while conquering Egypt before he became Emperor Augustas, the mausoleum was built in the Campus Martius.

Above:

Piazza Navona

Carabinieri in the Piazza Navona. The plethora of mopeds in Rome—and the increase in their use by petty thieves—is neatly countered by their use by the carabinieri, who patrol Rome's streets 24 hours a day.

Above:

Palazzo Farnese

The ceiling of the gallery within the Palazzo Farnese bears witness to the building's Renaissance origins. Architect
Antonio da Sangallo the Younger (d.1546) spent a great deal of time working on St. Peter's
in the Vatican before turning his attentions to this palace, the largest and most splendid of its type.
Michelangelo, who designed parts of it and finished much of the palace after Sangallo's death,
was dismissive of his predecessor for having a limited imagination.

Left:

Palazzo di Montecitorio

In Rome's political heartland lies the Palazzo di Montecitorio, designed by Bernini but completed in 1697 by Carl
Fontana. After unification it became the country's parliamentary chamber. Before the building stands an Egyptian
obelisk unearthed by Pope Benedict XIV (reigned 1740–58) and put up on this spot by Pius VI (reigned
1775–99) when the grand building still housed the Papal Tribune of Justice.

Above:

Palazzo di Santa Croce

Rome is renowned for its fountains. This one decorates the Palazzo di Santa Croce in Gerusalemme in the
Lateran district. The square takes its name from the nearby church founded in 320AD by St. Helena, the revered
mother of Constantine the Great. Its purpose was to house relics retrieved from the Holy Land by St. Helena
including thorns from Christ's crown, bits of his cross, and the finger of the doubting apostle St. Thomas.

Right:

Palazzo Zuccari

This imaginative yawning doorway is situated in the Palazzo Zuccari, named for the artist brothers Taddeo and
Federico Zuccari who were leading figures in Roman mannerism.

Above and Previous page:

Pantheon

The Pantheon, originally built by Agrippa in the reign of Augustus, was modeled into its present impressive
format by the Emperor Hadrian (reigned 117–38AD). Its extraordinary dome is considered to be one
of the major feats of ancient Roman engineering. Today it is a church housing the remains of Victor
Emmanuel II, Umberto I, and Raphael.

Right:

Piazza Barberini

Triton — the Greek sea god who is half human, half dolphin — perches upon a mighty scallop shell which is held
aloft by the tails of four obliging dolphins. He holds a giant conch from which water spurts. This fountain was
Bernini's project, executed in 1642 on behalf of Pope Urban VIII, one of the powerful Barberini family.
Indeed, it sits at the center of Piazza Barberini.

Above:

Piazza del Campidoglio

This most ancient of Roman sites stands testament not only to Michelangelo's architectural genius,
but also to the city's political and religious history. The Palazzo Senatorio, home to the mayoral offices,
now occupies the spot once occupied by the city's public records office; the Palazzo Nuovo,
to the left of the picture, houses one of the Capitoline's museums.

Above:

Piazza Farnese

Even amidst the faded beauty of ancient Rome, life goes on: a news stand does brisk business in the Piazza Farnese.

Above:
Piazza del Popolo

Work began on the Piazza del Popolo in 1816, so its fountains all date from afterward. As well as this elaborate fountain the Piazza is also famous for its marble lions standing at the foot of an ancient obelisk spewing water.

Right:
Piazza del Popolo

Although the Piazza is overshadowed by two churches — Santa Maria dei Miracoli and Santa Maria di Montesanto — it was here that many of Rome's public executions once took place. Men were killed either by *mazza* (hammer) or guillotine, often as part of carnival celebrations.

Above:
Piazza di Siena

The Piazza di Siena lies in the calm splendor of the Villa Borghese. Historically a racing site, equestrian events of the 1960 Rome Olympics were held there.

Above:
Piazza di Spagna

The Piazza di Spagna rests at the base of the Spanish Steps, brought alive here by azaleas in full bloom. For several centuries this has been the place to which all tourist routes lead in Rome. Horse-drawn carriages await passers by in the square.

Above:

Piazza della Minerva

Bernini designed this exquisite marble elephant in the Piazza della Minerva. The obelisk on its back comes from ancient Egypt and dates back from the sixth century BC. It was found in the back garden of the monastery of Santa Maria sopra Minerva nearby.

Right:

Piazza Mattei

The elegance of the 16th century Fontana delle Tartarughe (Tortoise) in the Piazza Mattei is an enormous attraction to visitors to the old Ghetto who are entranced by the graceful lines of the dolphins acting as footstools to the bronze youths supporting the top dish. The tortoises perched on the rim of dish were added later, possibly by Bernini.

Above:

Piazza di Trevi

This long view of the Piazza di Trevi shows the extent to which the Trevi Fountain fills the square—indeed the whole area has become a viewing gallery for the fountain. Crowds of people regularly line its rim, and the sheer scale and impact of it is enough to turn tourists' heads for a while from the architectural beauty all around them.

Overleaf:

Piazza Navona

On the ruins of a stadium built by the Emperor Domitian in 86AD stands the charming Piazza Navona. While it has three fountains and is bordered by numerous palaces the piazza is probably best known for its outdoor cafés.

Above & Right:
Shopping in Rome
The streets of Rome are packed with shops, many of which are geared to the tourist. They range from the quieter side streets to the busy and exclusive Via Condotti (right), where crowds of people browse shop windows in the shadow of the Spanish Steps.

Above:

Spanish Steps

Lazing away the afternoons on the Spanish Steps is a popular pastime for Romans and tourists alike. The steps, linking the French Church of Trinita dei Monti with the Piazza di Spagna, were completed in 1726 after a graceful design by Italian architect Francesco de Sanctis bridged the gulf between the pope and the French authorities.

Right:

Spanish Steps

At the foot of the Spanish Steps lies the Fontana della Baraccia, providing pleasing entertainment for the tourists who perch on the cascading steps to soak up the city's abundant atmosphere.

Above, Right, and Overleaf:

St. Peter's

Built on the arena used by Nero for the torment of Christians, it is said St. Peter was crucified here, upside down, and St. Paul beheaded. The first basilica on the site was dedicated in 326AD under the direction of Emperor Constantine. Its replacement is the one still standing today, a triumph of Renaissance design. The distinctive dome was the brainchild of Michelangelo. Already into his seventies by the time he took charge of the project he died before it was completed. Other eminent architects associated with St. Peter's during the 150 years it took to complete include Bramante, Raphael, Antonio da Sangallo, Giacomo della Porta, and Carlo Marderno. No matter how hot the weather the dress code for St. Peter's remains rigorously enforced. Shorts are strictly forbidden for both men and women. Mini skirts are likewise banned and so are bare chests and shoulders.

Above:

Temple of Mars

Standing close to the Forum, the Temple of Mars was approached by a sweeping stairway that had fountains to either side. The remains of three of its original eight massive columns can still be seen.

Right:

Tempietto

To some it is the first Renaissance building in Rome. Bramante replicated the early Christian chapels in design for it is here that St. Peter is believed to have been crucified. It echoes the classical glory of Rome which was in part revived in the Renaissance.

Previous page:

St. Peter's

The Vatican and specifically, the pope, is under the protection of the Swiss Guards. Brightly costumed in red, yellow and blue, the 100 Guards are nonetheless highly trained soldiers seasoned in using their 15th century pikes. The Guards were established in 1506 by Pope Julius II. Their efficacy is under question in today's world of sophisticated firearms. Yet it would be hard to find more devoted and physically fit men for the task.

Above:

Temple of Castor and Pollux

Among the most striking ruins of the Forum are the columns that remain of the Temple of Castor and Pollux. It was dedicated to the mythical twins now associated with the Gemini birth sign after they allegedly appeared on the battlefield to spur on the republicans against the deposed Tarquin kings in 496BC. Of course, the original building is mostly gone. The columns date from 12BC when the Temple was last rebuilt following a fire.

Right:

Church of Santa Luce e Martina

Vespasian (7–79AD) was the emperor who acted decisively to end the civil war that prevailed in Rome when he came to power in 69AD. After his death he was deified and a magnificent temple was dedicated to him. Alas, most of it has crumbled and only these columns remain. In the background lies the medieval church Santa Luca e Martina.

Previous page:

Temple of Antonius and Faustina

The Temple of Antonius and Faustina lies in the Forum. It was built by Antonius himself to honor his wife on her death in 141AD. When he died 20 years later his name was added to the architrave. In the Middle Ages the Temple became a church, San Lorenzo in Miranda.

Above:
Temple of Vesta

This beautiful, serene building once housed the sacred fire of the city, which was originally tended by the daughters of the king. Later the task fell to six priestesses known as Vestals. These women were chosen from the patrician class at the age of six and a part of their duty was to maintain their virginity for the 30 years that they spent in the temple. Failure to do so incurred terrible punishment. Vestal virgins who were found to have broken their vow were buried alive on the Quirnal Hill.

Right and Overleaf:
River Tiber

Rising in the Apennines, the Tiber — or Tevere as it is known in Italy — runs south for 405km (252 miles), scything through Rome before exiting in the Tyrrhenian Sea at Ostia. The river has been in constant use since the earliest days of the city, providing as it does a link to both the inner heartland of Italy as well as the trade routes of the Mediterranean Sea. High embankments on either side of the river were built very early in Rome's history due to frequent flooding.

Above:

River Tiber

One of Italy's longest rivers the Tiber held the key to much of the city's dominance in ancient history. Named after King Tiberinus of Alba Longa, its place in history was sealed when Romulus and Remus were set afloat on it.

Right:

Transport

A couple share a motor scooter. This breezy and inexpensive form of transport has become the favorite of Romans. They can be seen everywhere and constitute terrifying moving obstacles for brave pedestrians all over Rome. Piaggio is the main Italian manufacturer, and their scooters are perfectly suited to Rome's often narrow and cobbled streets, and car-blocked main roads.

Above & Right:
Traffic

Traffic at a standstill in front of the monument to Victor Emmanuel II in the Piazza Venezia (above), and police-men directing traffic (right). Driving in Italy is considered a somewhat dangerous pastime, advisable only for the practiced. Accident rates are high and motor scooters to be watched out for as they hurtle through traffic.

Above and Right:
Trevi Fountain

The Trevi Fountain, built in 1762 on the site of the much earlier Aqua Virgo aqueduct, was made famous — or notorious — when Anita Ekberg plunged into it for the film *La Dolce Vita*. Legend has it that visitors who throw a coin into its waters are guaranteed to return. Neptune is the central figure of the fountain. The son of Saturn and the brother of Jupiter and Pluto, Neptune was originally the god of springs and streams until Roman culture absorbed that of the Greeks. Thereafter he became associated with Poseidon, the Greek god of the sea.

Previous page:
Trajan's Market

Trajan (reigned 98–117AD) styled himself as "the new Caesar" and had great ambitions at home and overseas. But his greatest legacy was the market place that took his name. Military engineer Apollodorus of Damascus was responsible for its construction and had the necessary site razed before work commenced. Within its boundaries is Trajan's Column, famous for its exquisite tale-telling reliefs.

Above:

Villa Farnesina

The Villa Farnesina was designed by the architect Baldassarre Peruzzi (1483–1536) from Siena after a commission by a wealthy banker, Agostino Chigi. The interior rivals its outer facades for sumptious style. It includes frescoes by Raphael, Sodoma, and Peruzzi himself.

Right:

Vatican Gardens

The Papal Gardens within the Vatican are a green lung for Rome, which extends beyond. Also within the city boundaries of the Vatican are St. Peter's Square, St. Peter's Basilica, and the Vatican Palace. There are also Vatican army and police services and Radio Vaticano, which provides up-to-the-minute Church news in 31 different languages.

Above:

Victor Emanuel Bridge

The Roman bridge named for Victor Emanuel II (1820–78), the king of Sardinia-Piedmont who fought for and won the unification of Italy alongside Garibaldi. He was king of all Italy from 1861 until his death.

Left:

Victor Emanuel II Monument

While Victor Emanuel II (1820–78) is revered in Rome for his success in unifying Italy, the monument to him completed in 1911 is not. It has been labeled as "the wedding cake" or "the typewriter" by disdainful locals. This gilt bronze statue of the king astride his steed atop a white marble block has limited appeal.

Above:

Vatican

A large crowd attend an audience with the Pope outside the Vatican, in the Piazza san Pietro.

Right:

Vatican: Swiss Guard

Two members of the Swiss Guard, the special guard of the pope, on duty at the Vatican. The Swiss Guard must be Swiss citizens, unmarried, and catholic. The design of their uniforms is attributed to Michelangelo; and though their halberds are symbolic of their defense role, they are trained in the use of firearms.

Above:
Villa Medici

The 16th century Villa Medici took its name from one of its early residents, Cardinal Ferdinando de Medici. In 1803 it became the venue for the French Academy, which had been founded in 1666 by Louis XIV for the training of painters. Once at the Villa Medici the Academy began to admit musicians and both Berlioz and Debussy studied there.

Left:
Roman Forum

Rainclouds darken the Coliseum, threatening the sunlit ruins of the Forum. The three columns to the right of the picture are the remains of the Temple of Castor and Pollux; they nearly conceal the Arch of Titus, behind. The Sacred Way, or Via Sacra, runs through the Forum, still lined with the remnants of colonnades. The steps and portico of the Temple of Antonius and Faustina are visible to the left of the picture.

INDEX